THE FAIRY RING

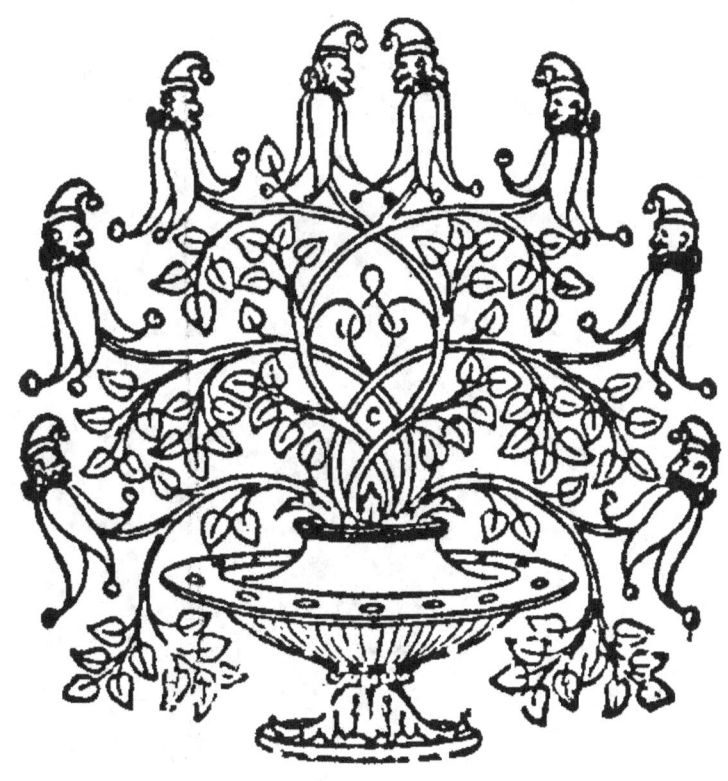

ILLUSTRATED BY ELIZABETH MACKINSTRY

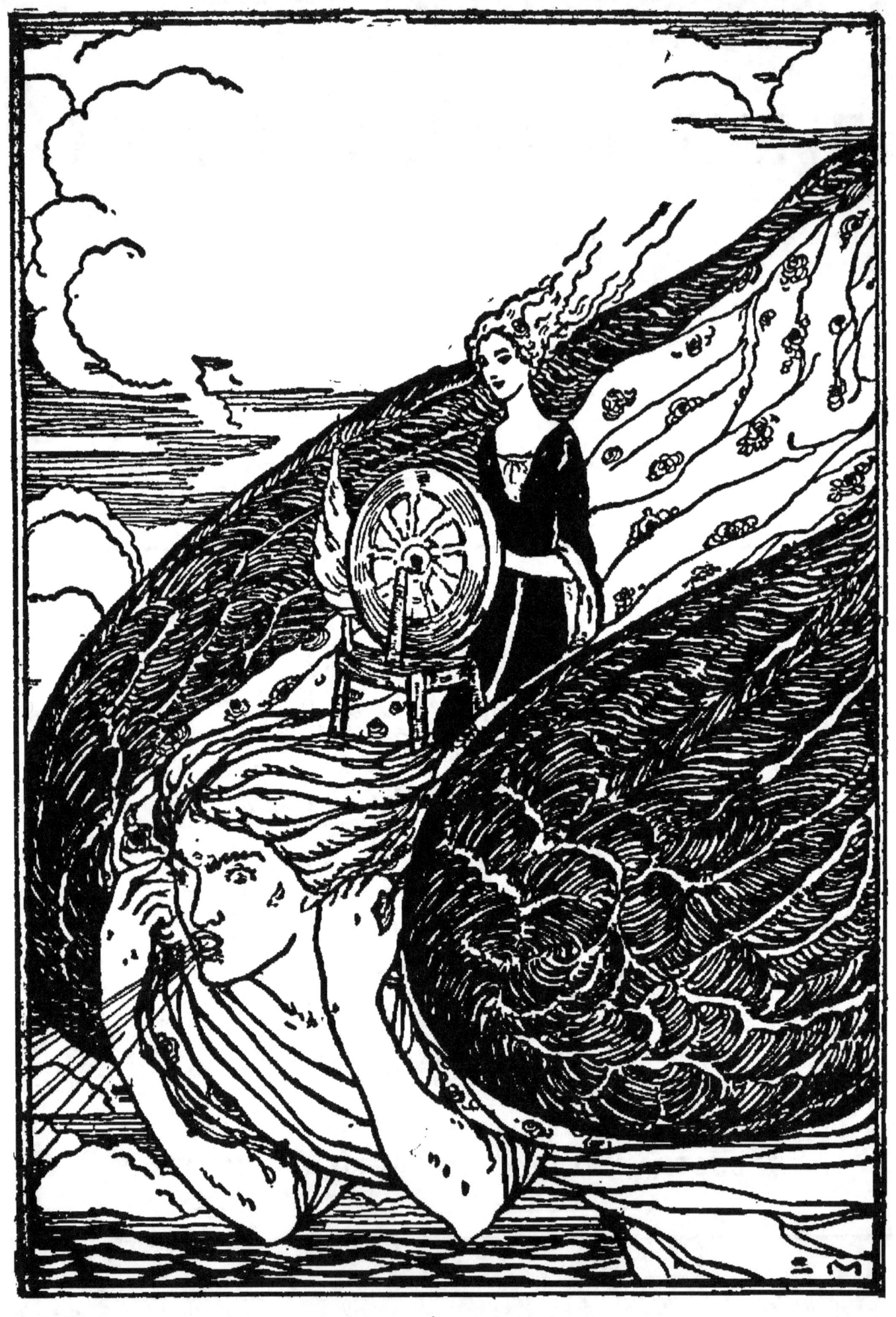

THE LASSIE RIDING OVER THE SEA ON THE BACK OF THE NORTH WIND

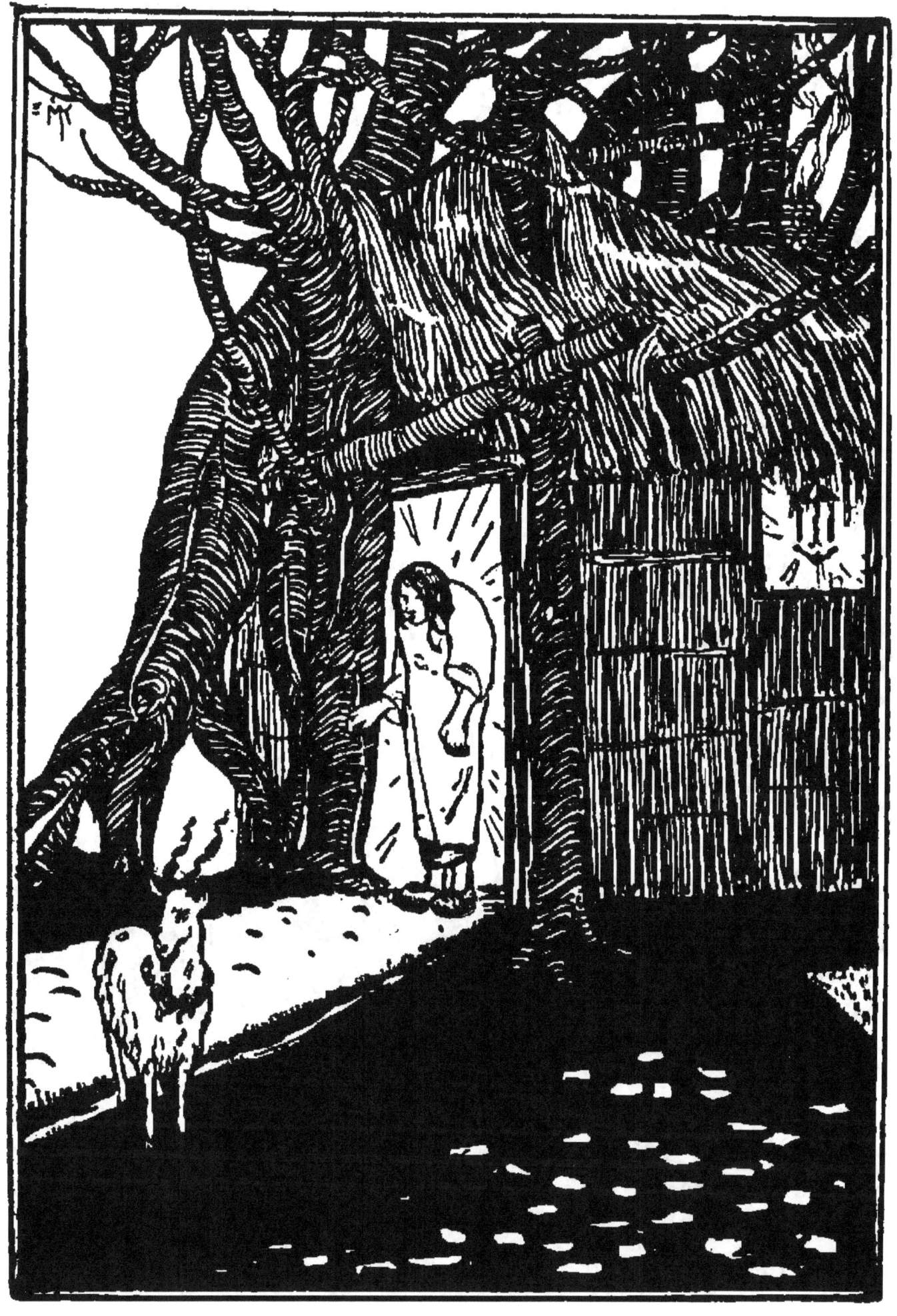

THE TROLL'S HUT, THE LANTERN, AND THE GOAT WITH THE GOLDEN HORNS

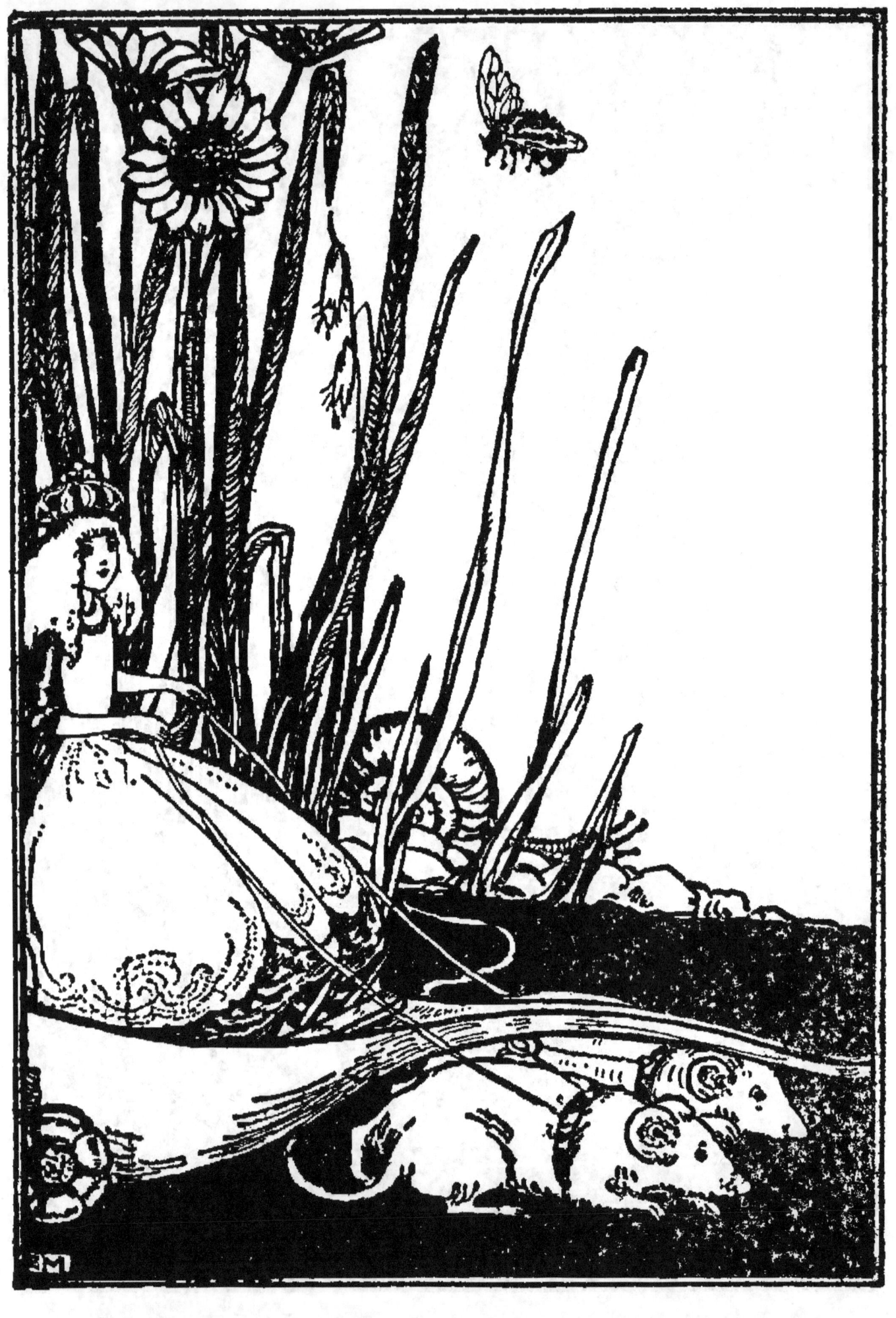

"SHE SAID SHE WOULD SIT AND DRIVE IN A SILVER SPOON"

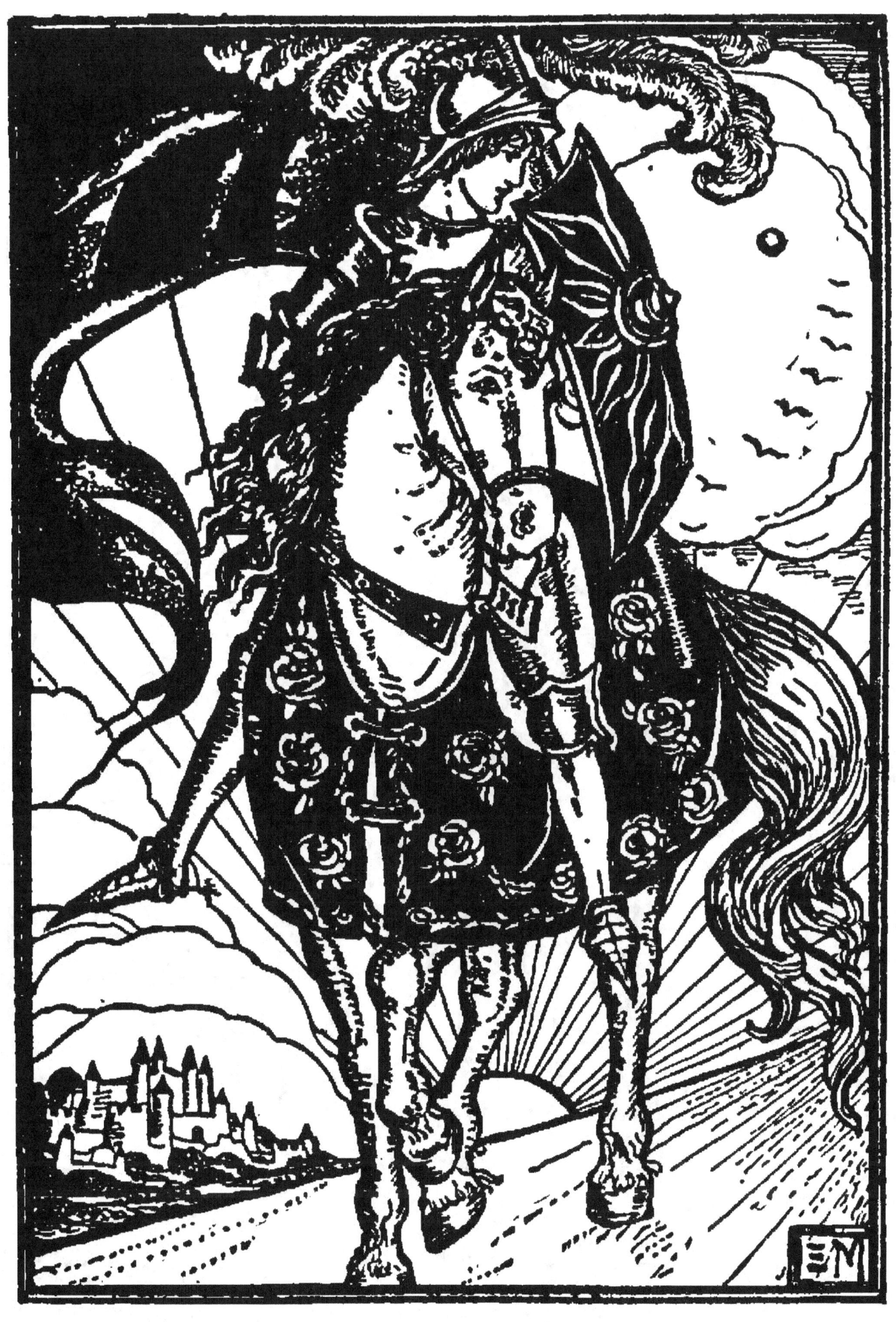

JUST AS CINDERLAD TURNED HIS HORSE AROUND, THE PRINCESS THREW THE GOLDEN APPLE

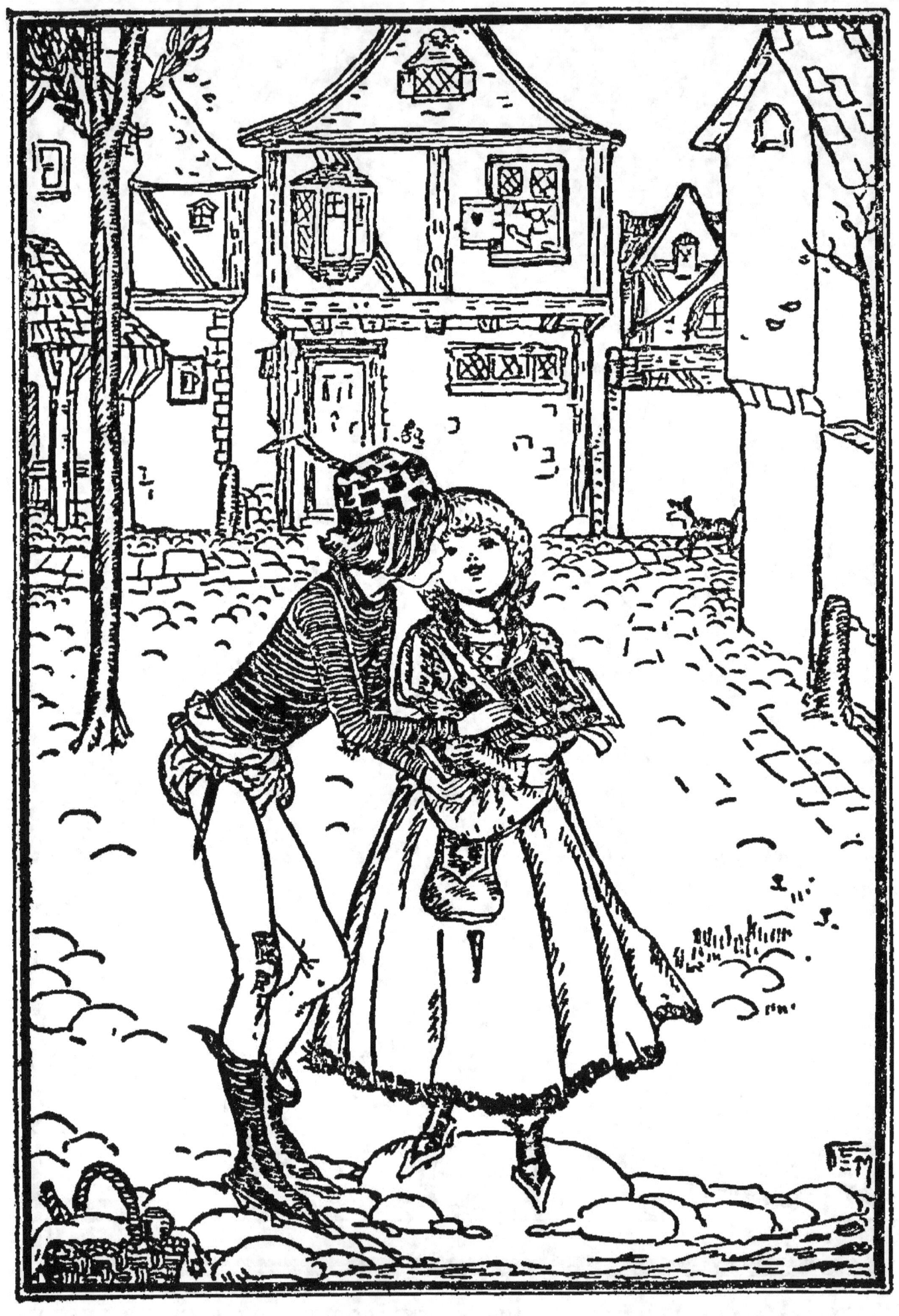

"AND WHEN HE SET HER DOWN HE GAVE HER A KISS"

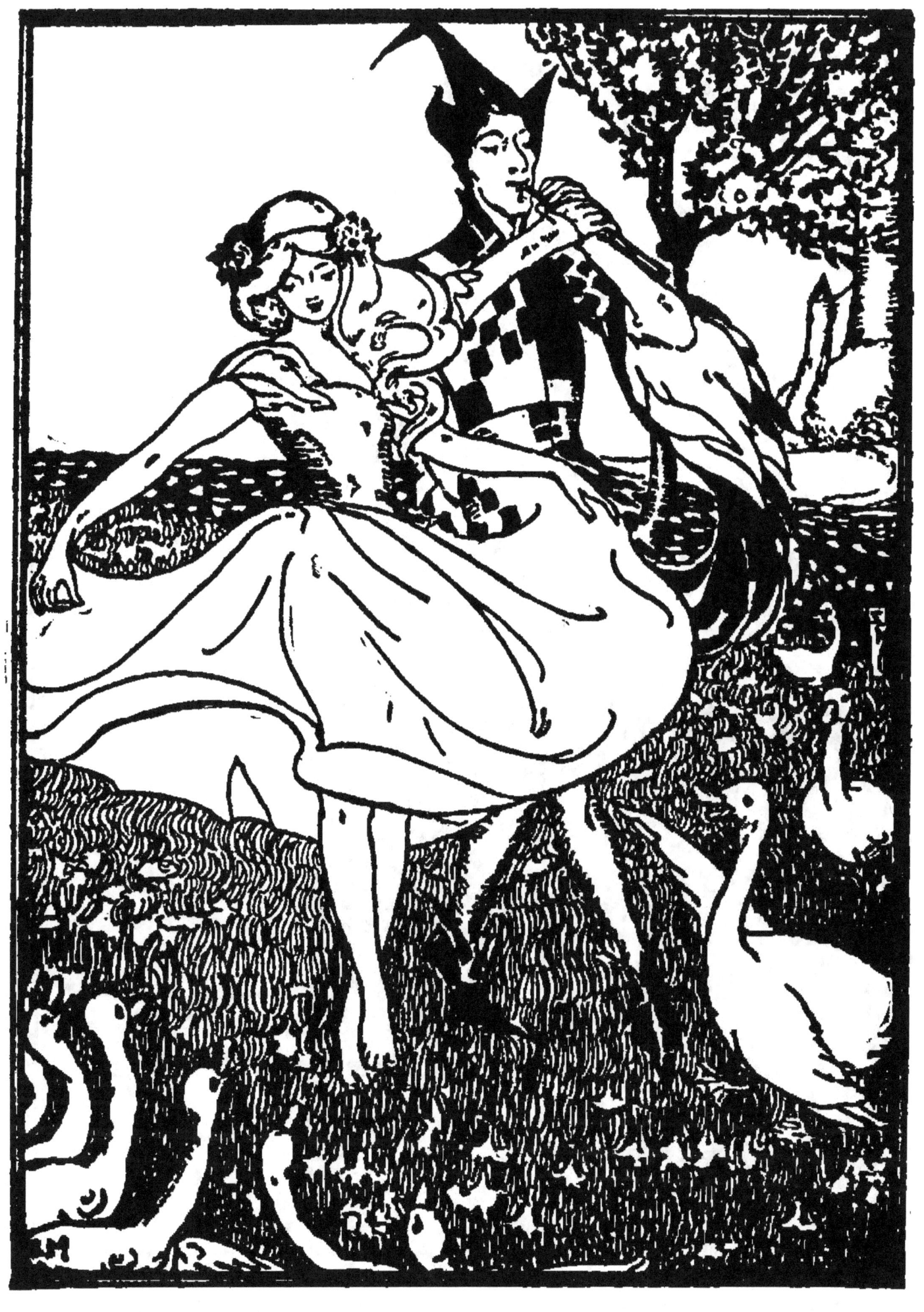

TATTERCOATS FORGOT ALL HER TROUBLES AND FELL TO DANCING

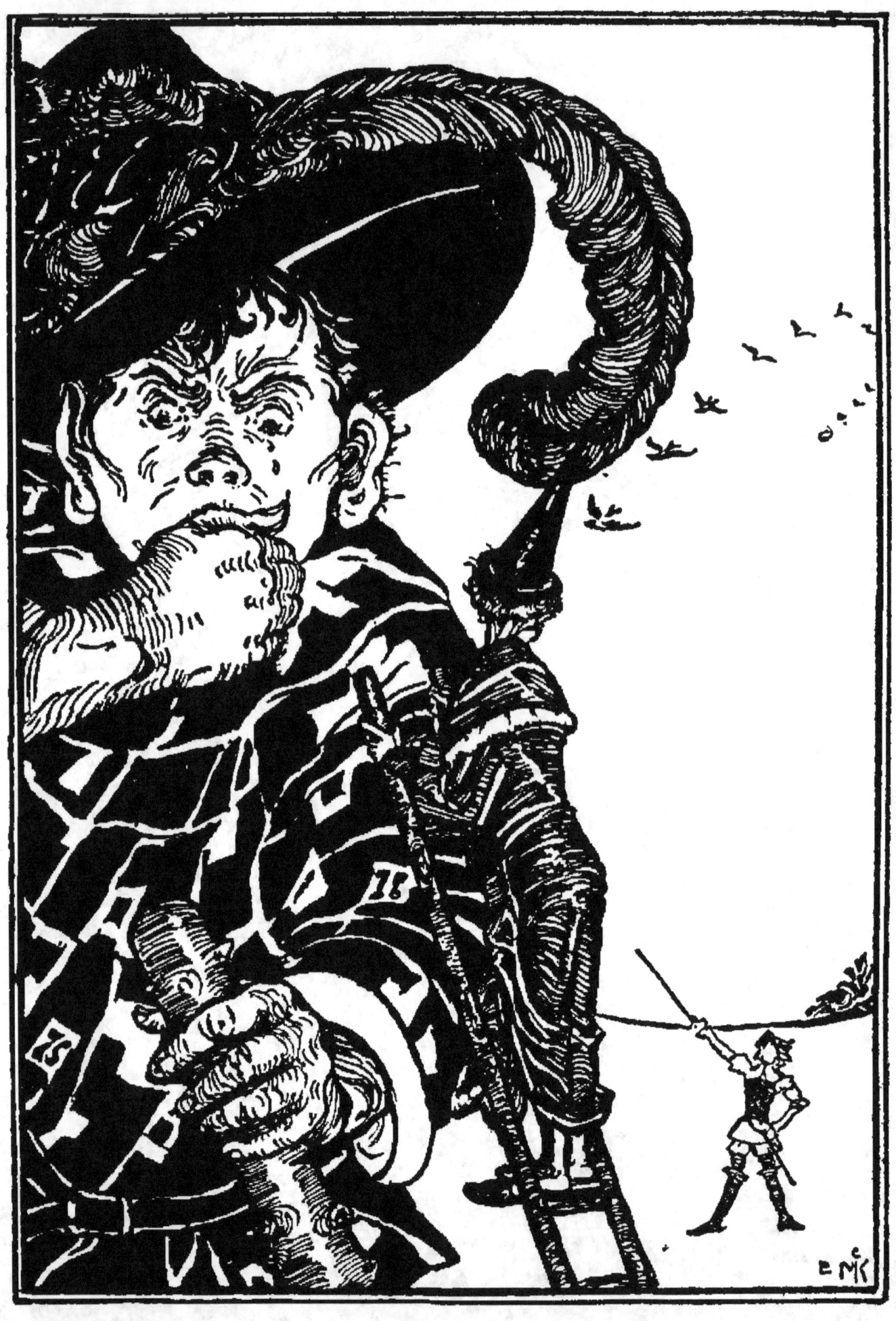

"THE GIANT AND THE CONJURER NOW KNEW THAT THEIR WICKED COURSE WAS AT AN END"

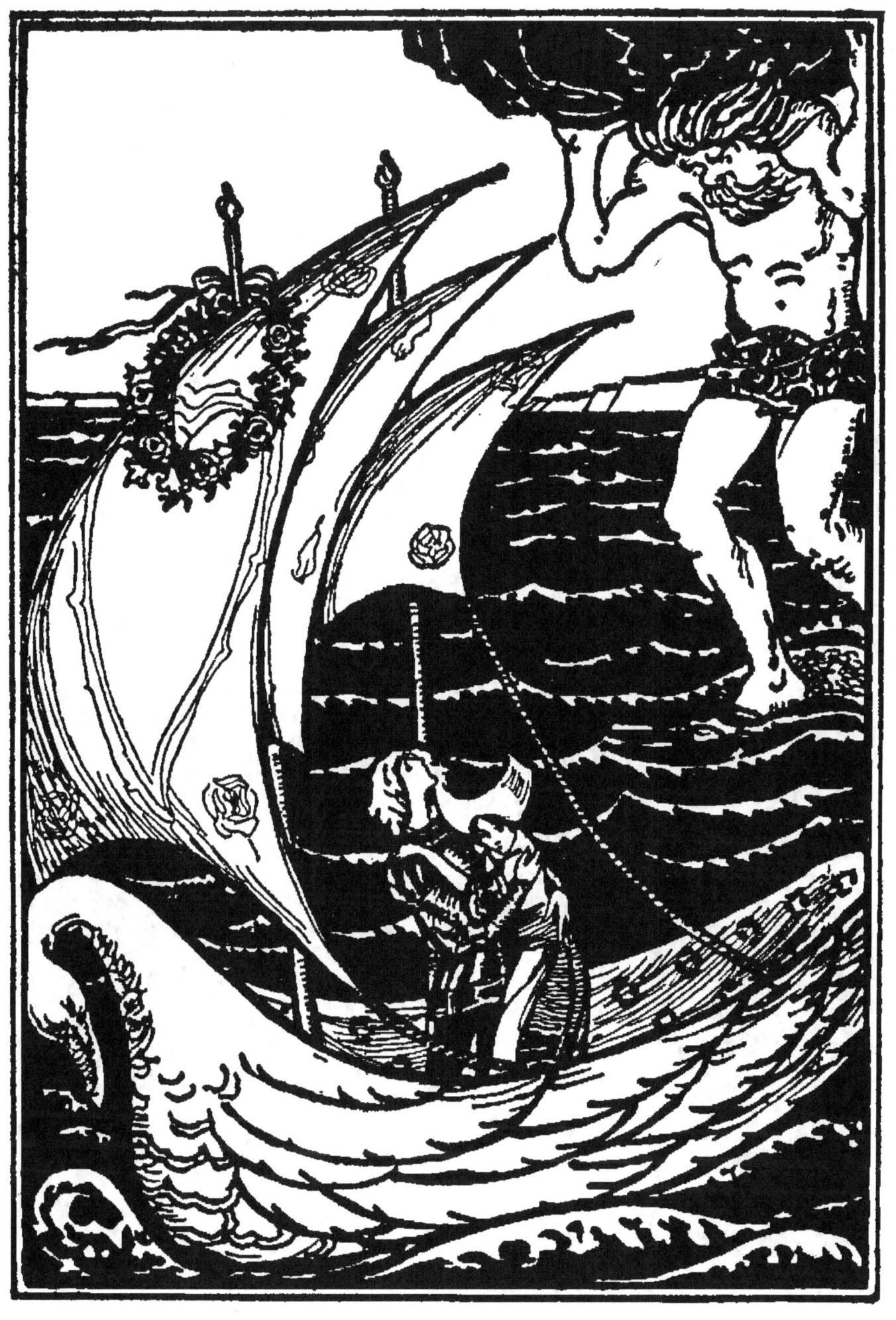

"HE FLUNG HUGE MASSES OF ROCK AFTER THE VESSEL"

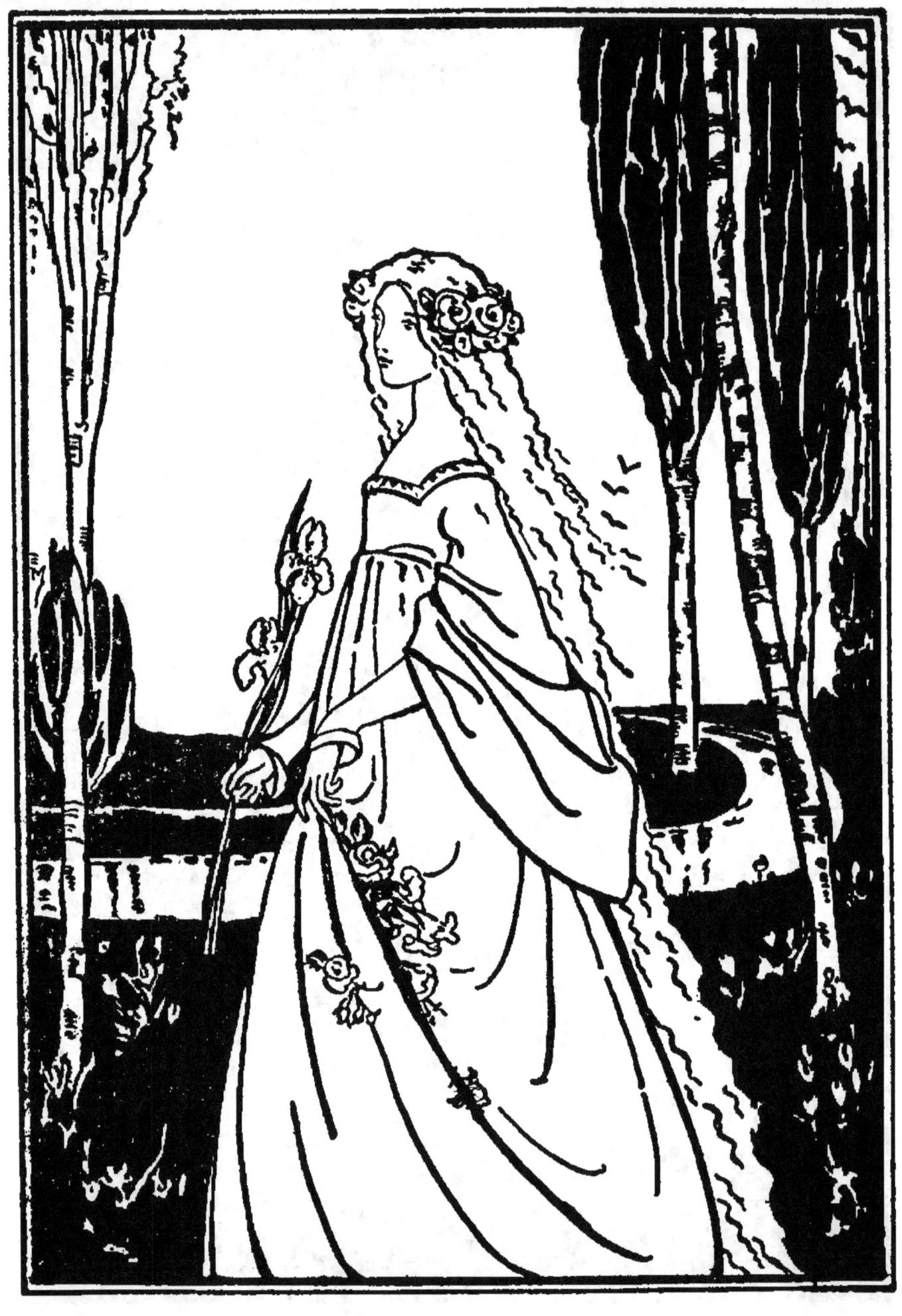

"SHE WORE THEM ALWAYS . . . LOOSE AND FLOWING"

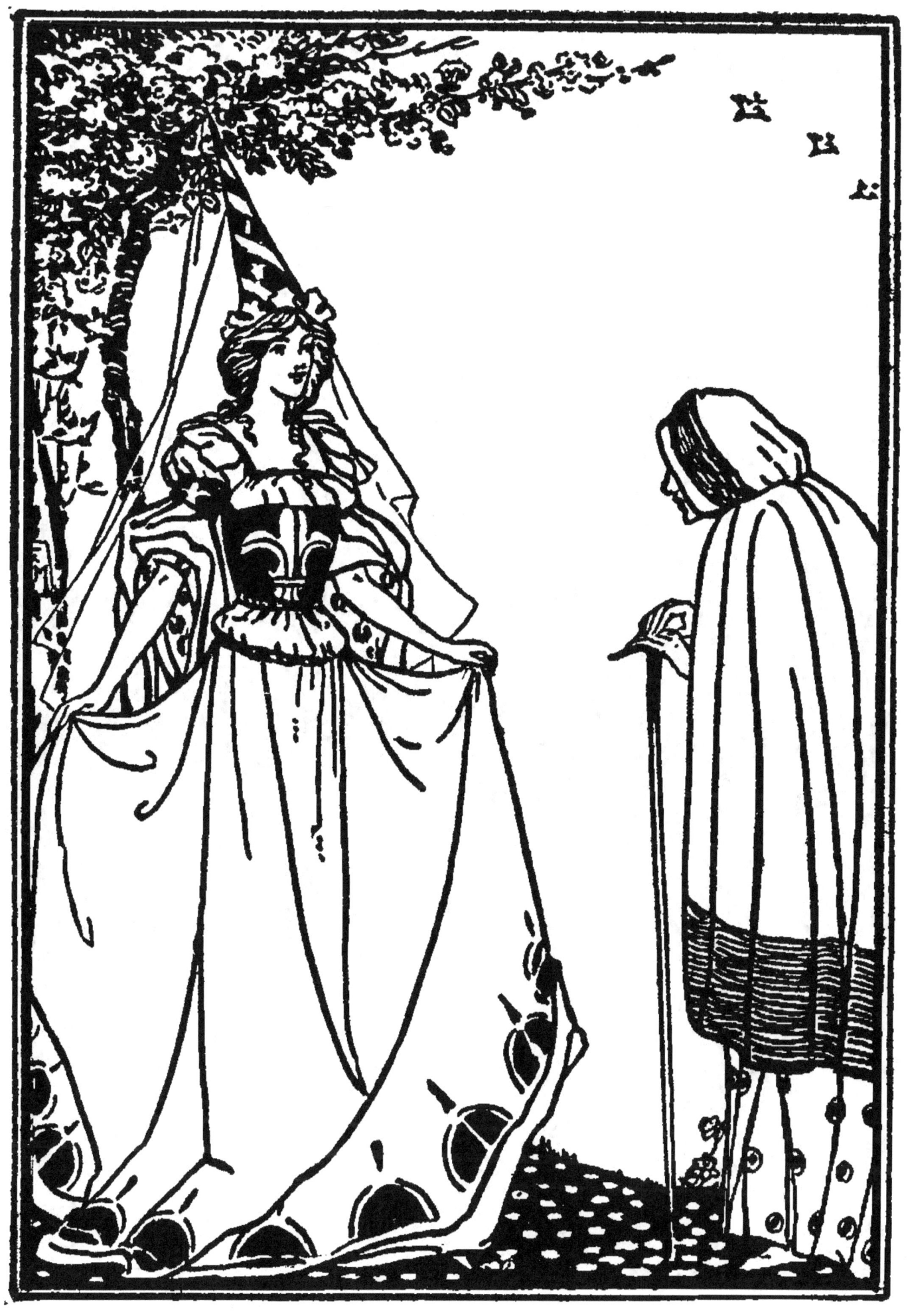
"I FEEL AS IF I WERE THE DAUGHTER OF SOME GREAT KING"

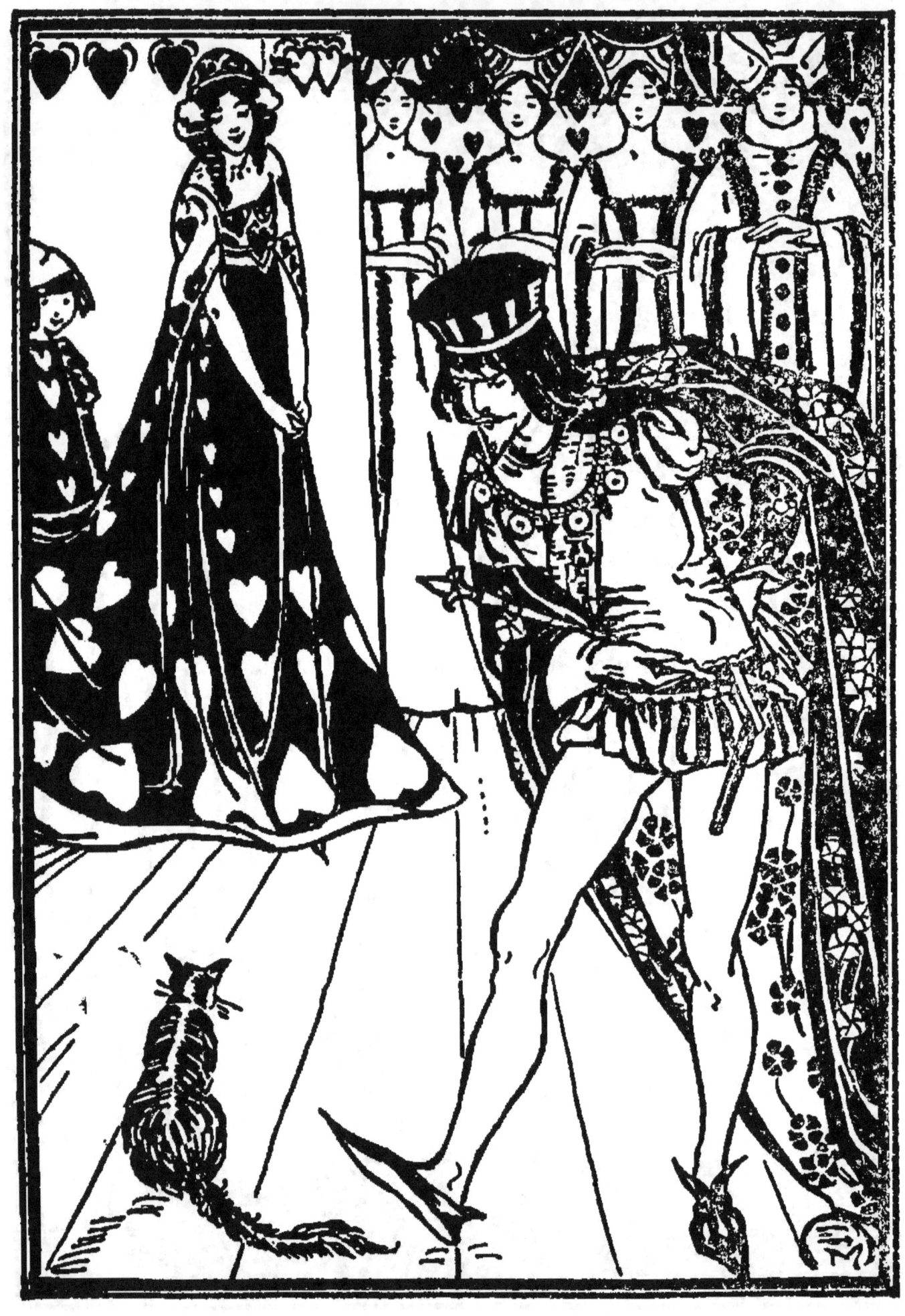

"HE WAS A WEEK TRYING TO TREAD ON THIS FATAL TAIL"

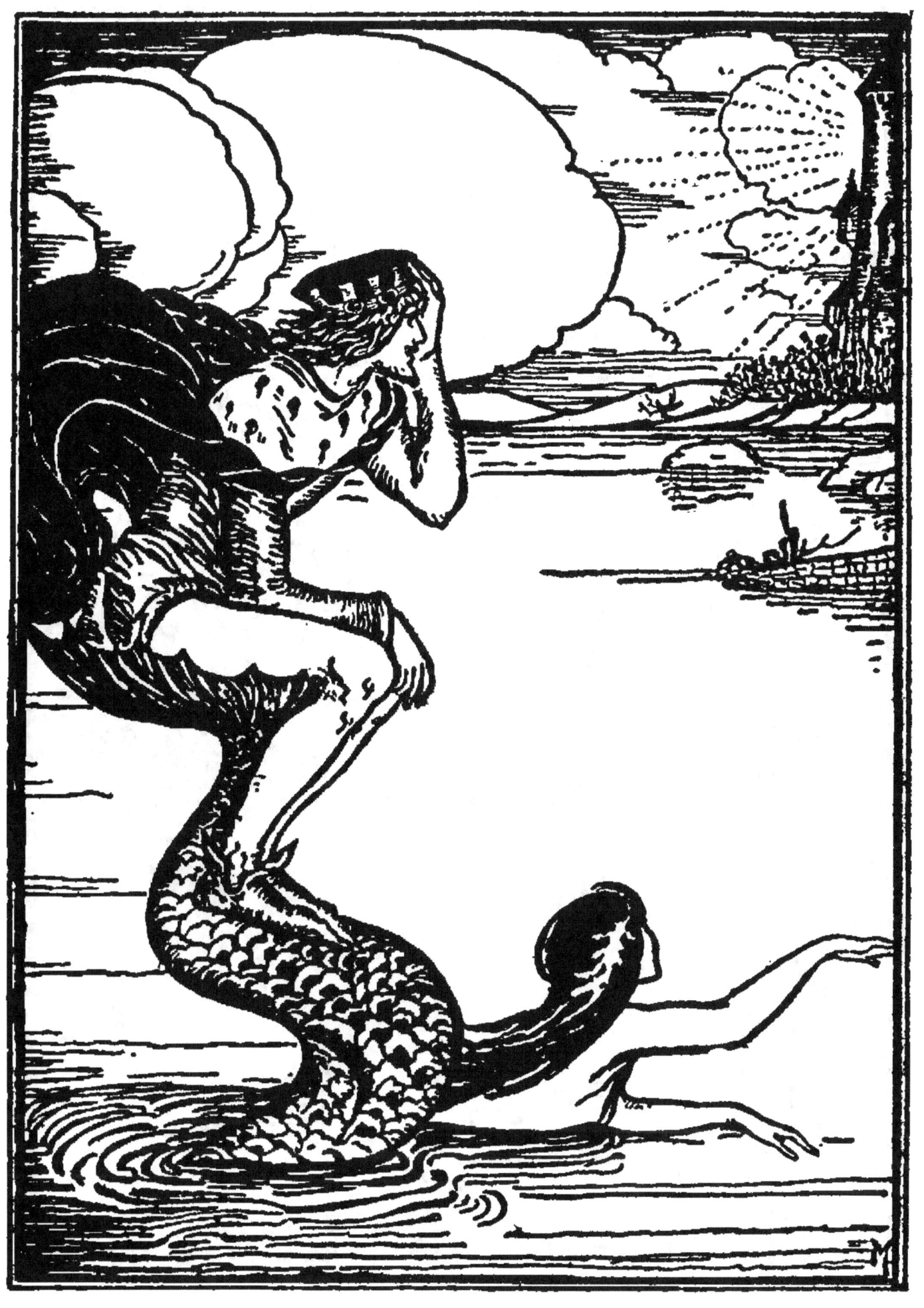
THE MERMAID TAKING THE KING OF THE GOLDEN MINES TO THE STEEL CASTLE

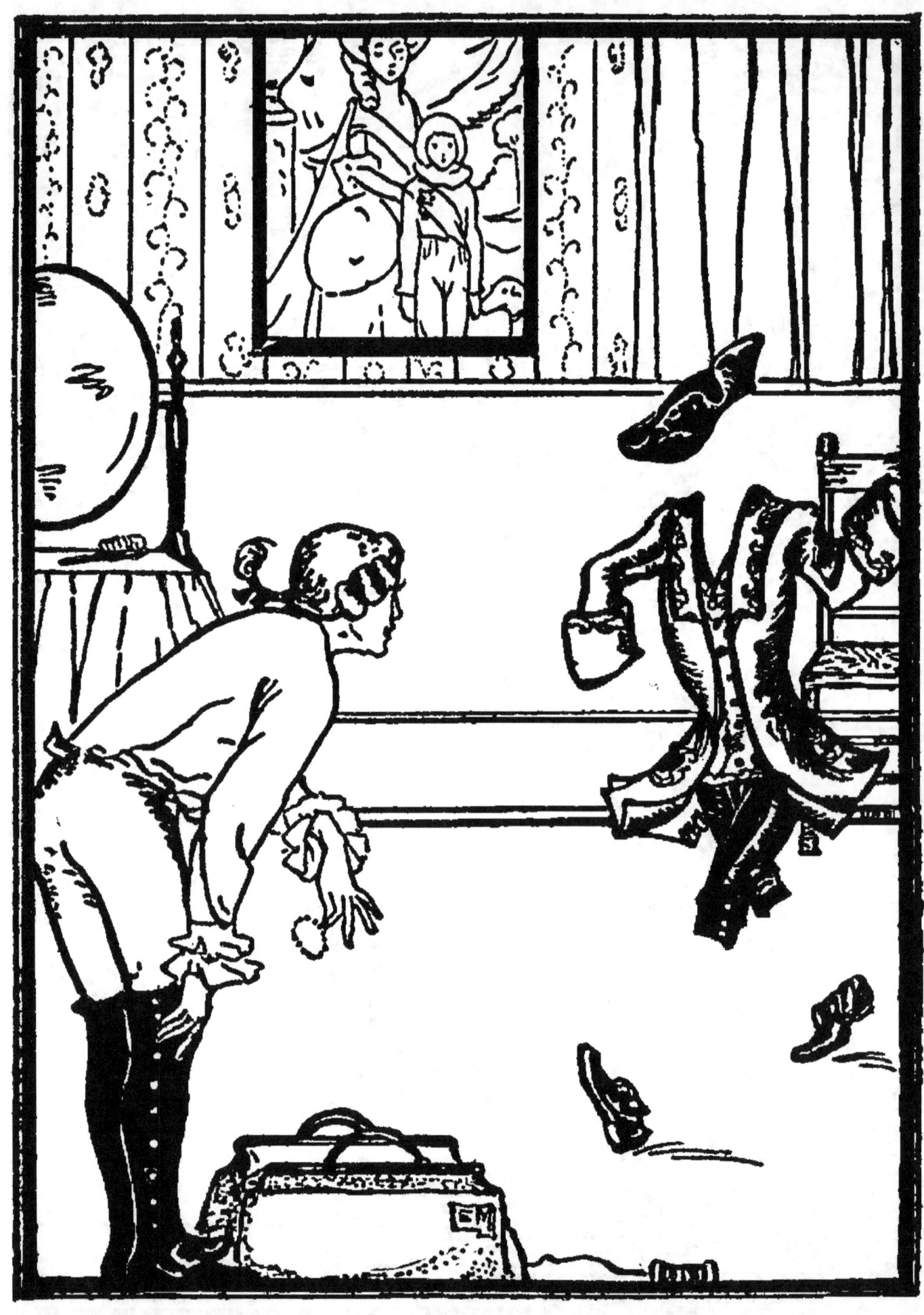

"MICHEAL, PETRIFIED, STOOD MUTE, . . . CONTEMPLATING WITH A FRIGHTENED AIR THIS INCONGRUOUS DANCE"

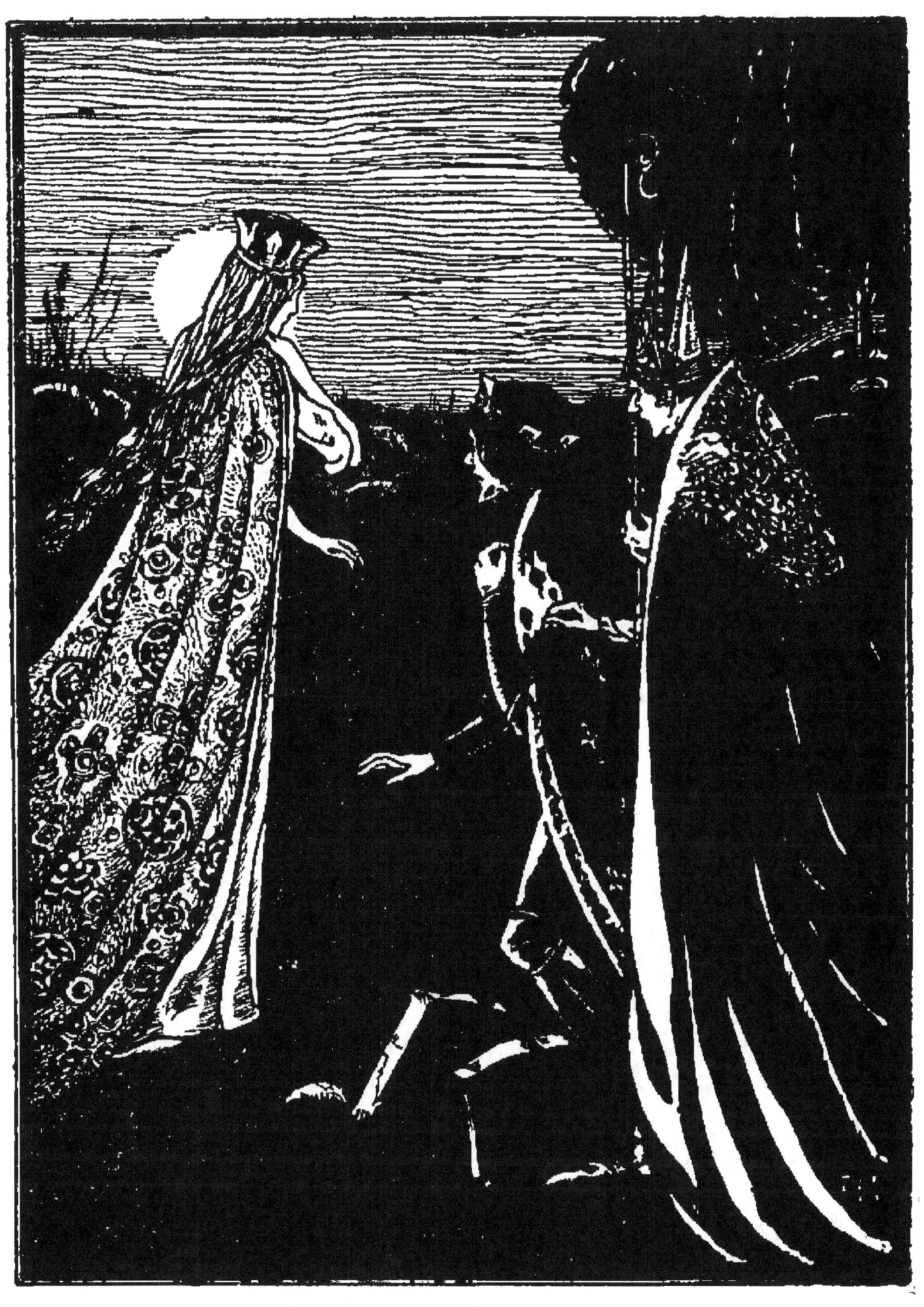

"ELIZA WENT, AND THE KING AND THE ARCHBISHOP FOLLOWED HER"

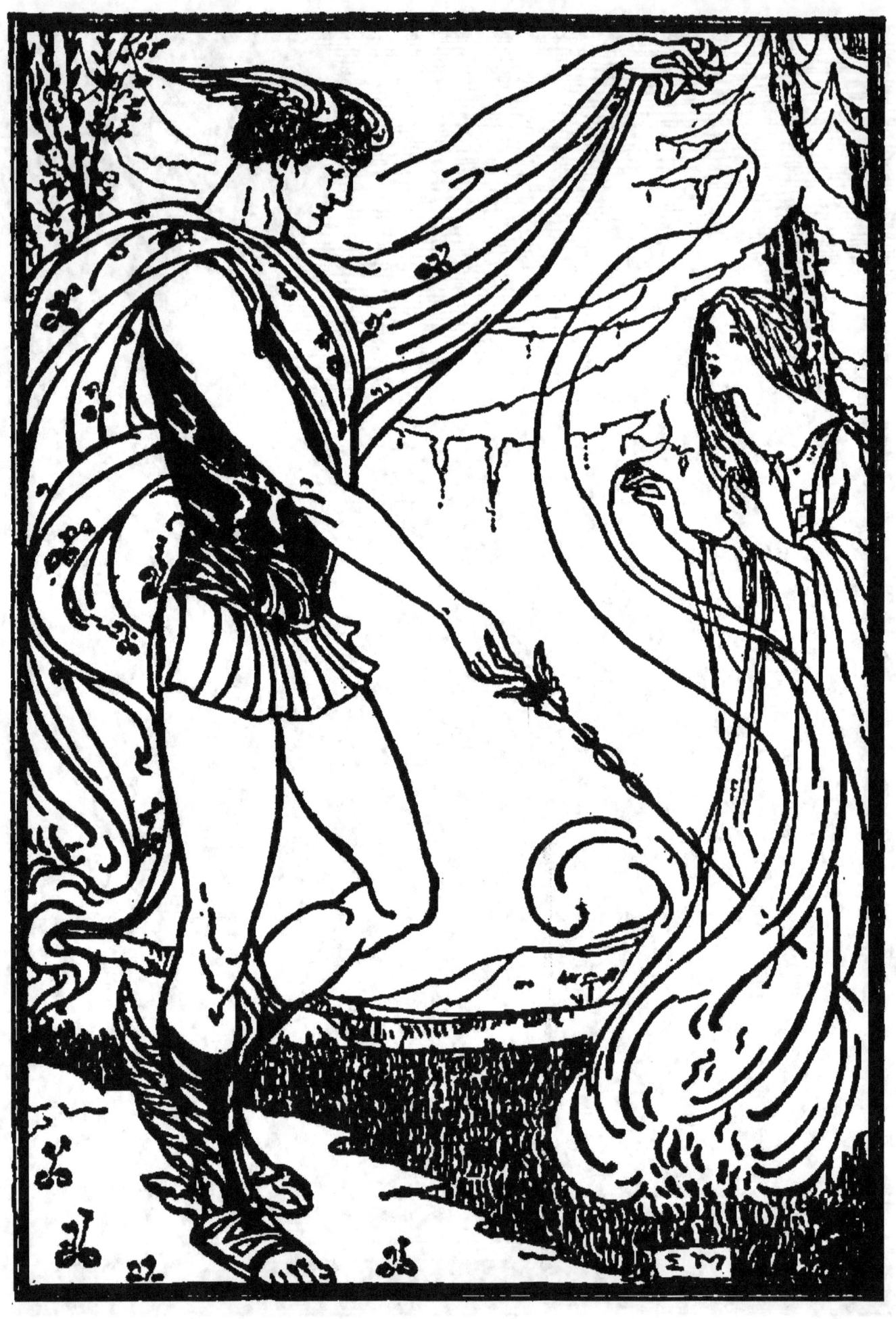

"MARCH ROSE IN TURN, AND STIRRED THE FIRE WITH THE STAFF, WHEN, BEHOLD! . . . IT WAS SPRING"

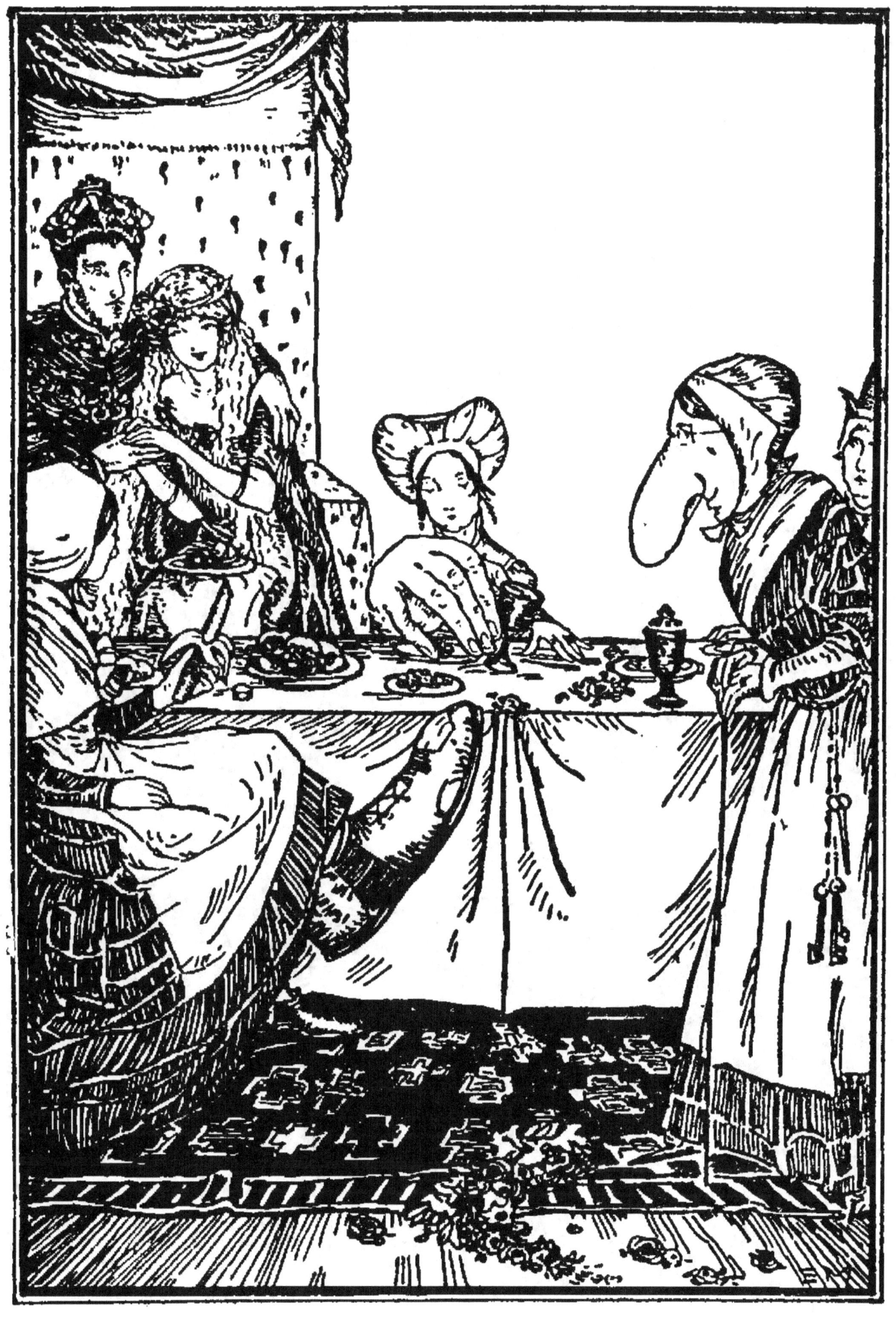
"AN UGLY OLD WOMAN WITH THE MOST MONSTROUS NOSE EVER BEHELD"

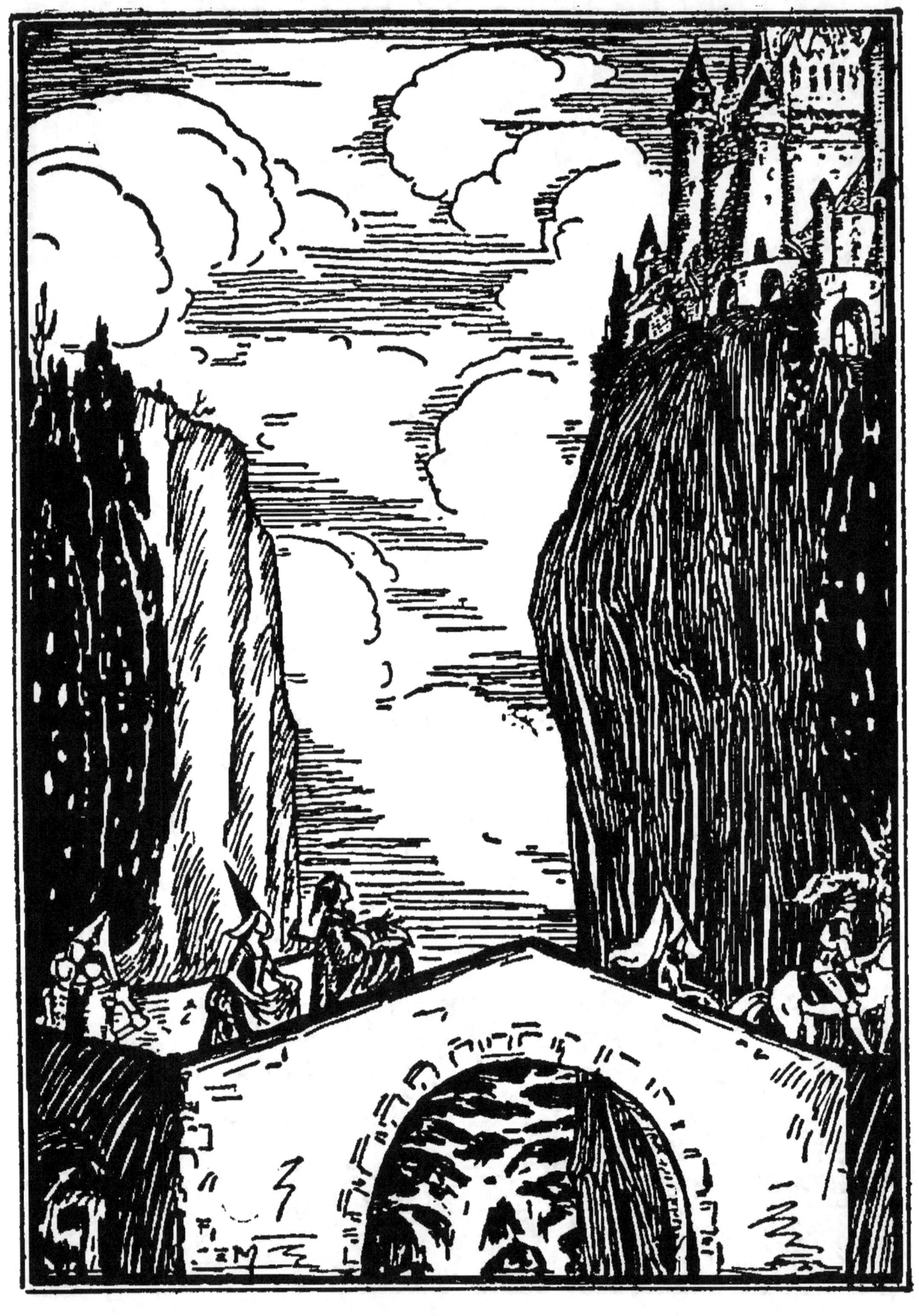
"IN THIS WAY THE FISHERMAN CARRIED HIM TO THE CASTLE"

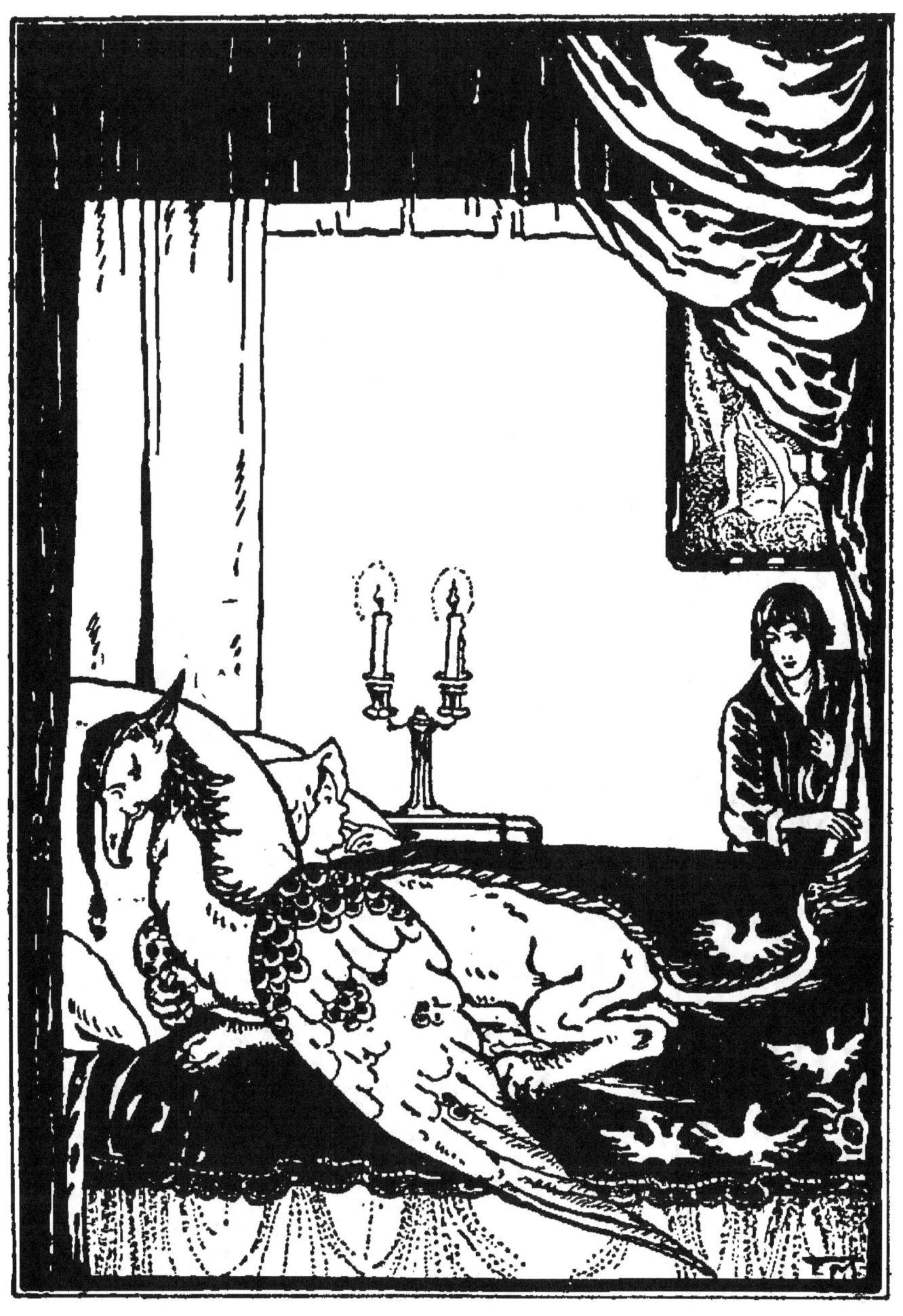

"IN THE MIDDLE OF THE NIGHT, WHEN GRIFFIN WAS SNORING AWAY LUSTILY, JACK REACHED UP AND PULLED A FEATHER OUT OF HIS TAIL"

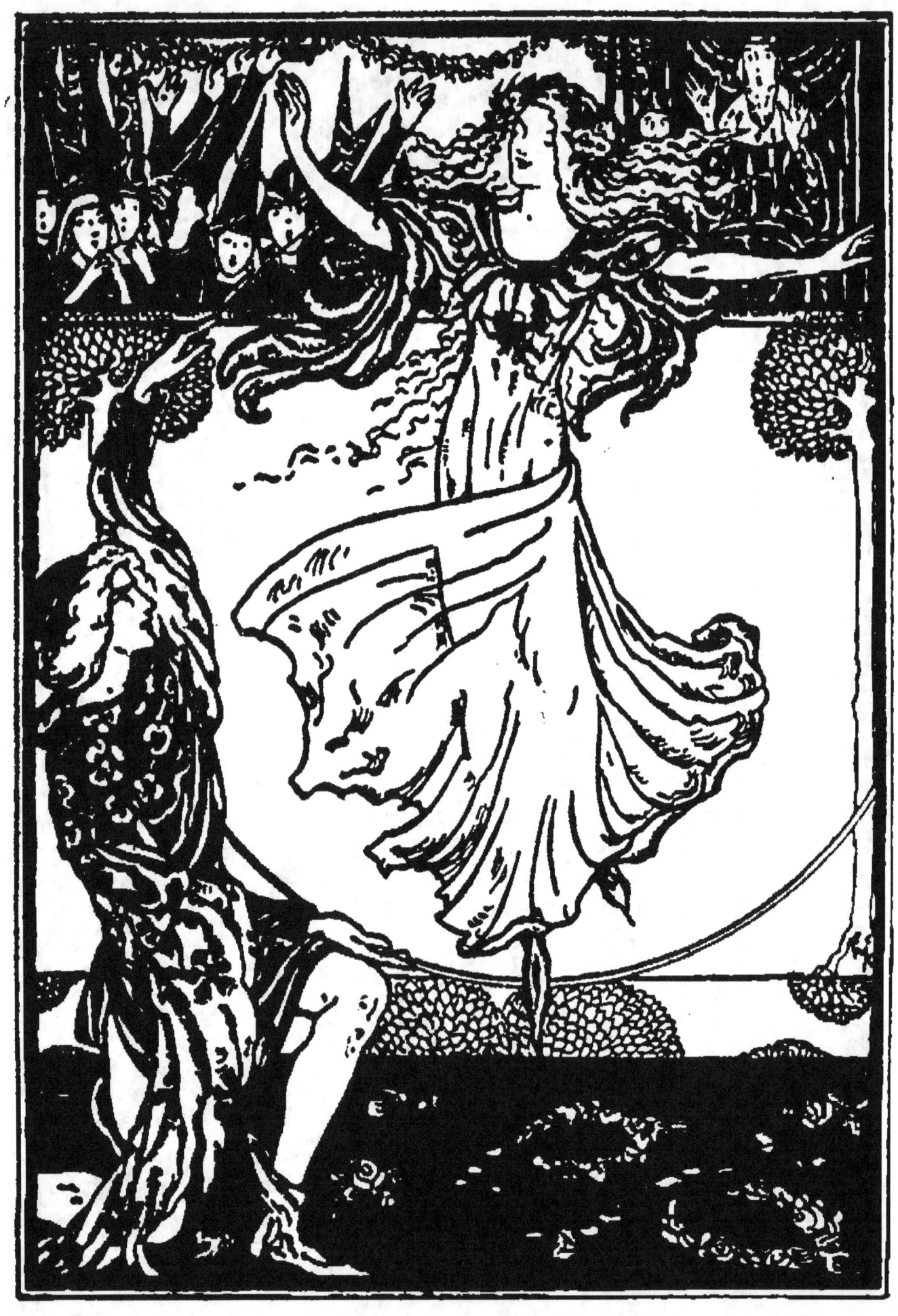

"THEN DUMMLING'S LOVELY MAIDEN SPRANG LIGHTLY AND GRACEFULLY THROUGH THE RING"

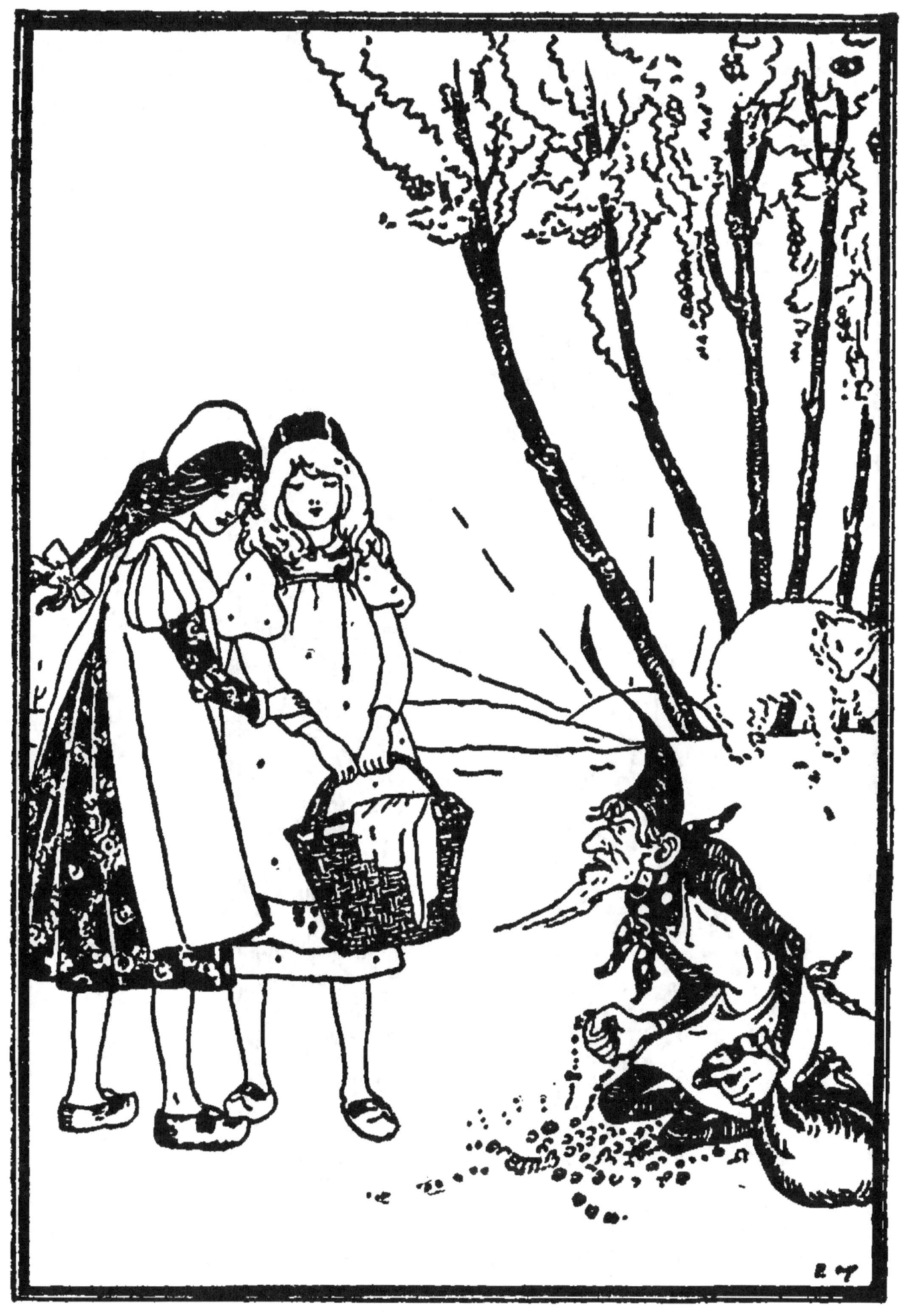
"'WHAT ARE YOU STANDING THERE GAPING FOR?' SCREAMED THE DWARF"

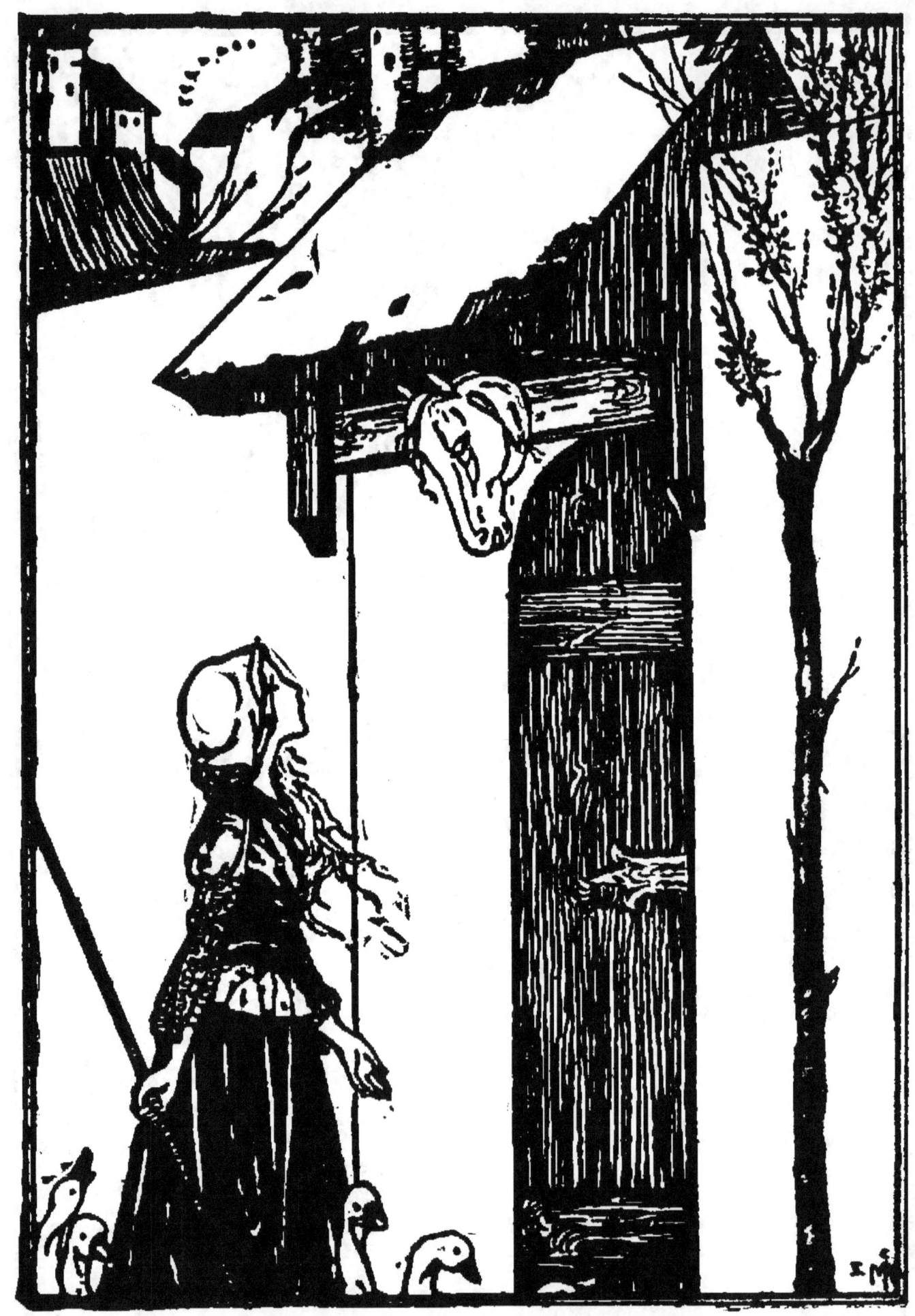

"FALADA, FALADA, THERE THOU HANGEST!"
"BRIDE, BRIDE, THERE THOU GANGEST!"

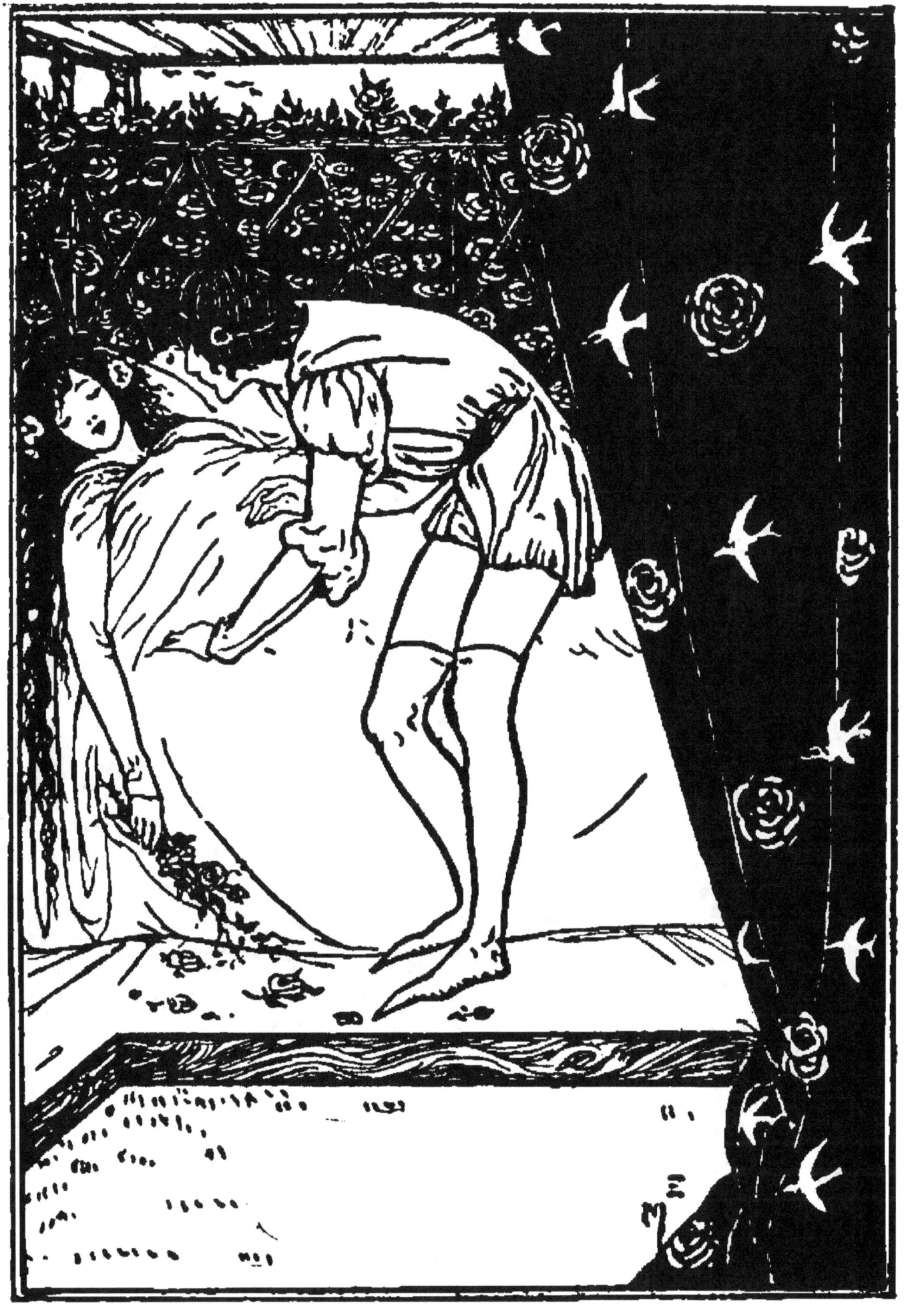

"AT LAST HE REACHED THE TOWER . . . WHERE BRIER ROSE WAS ASLEEP"

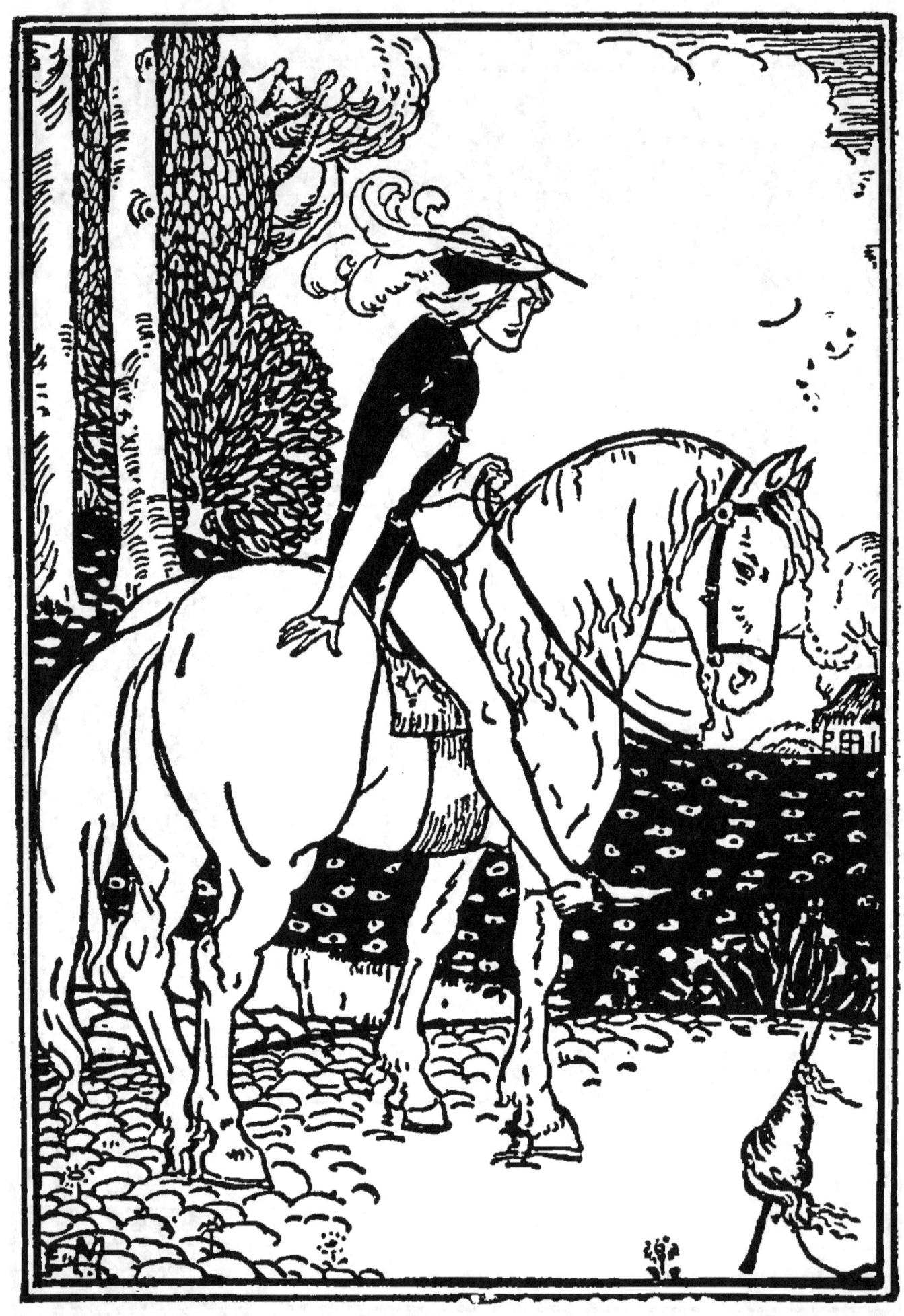

"JUST AS IT HAD COME TO THE END OF THE GOLDEN THREAD IT REACHED THE KING'S SON"

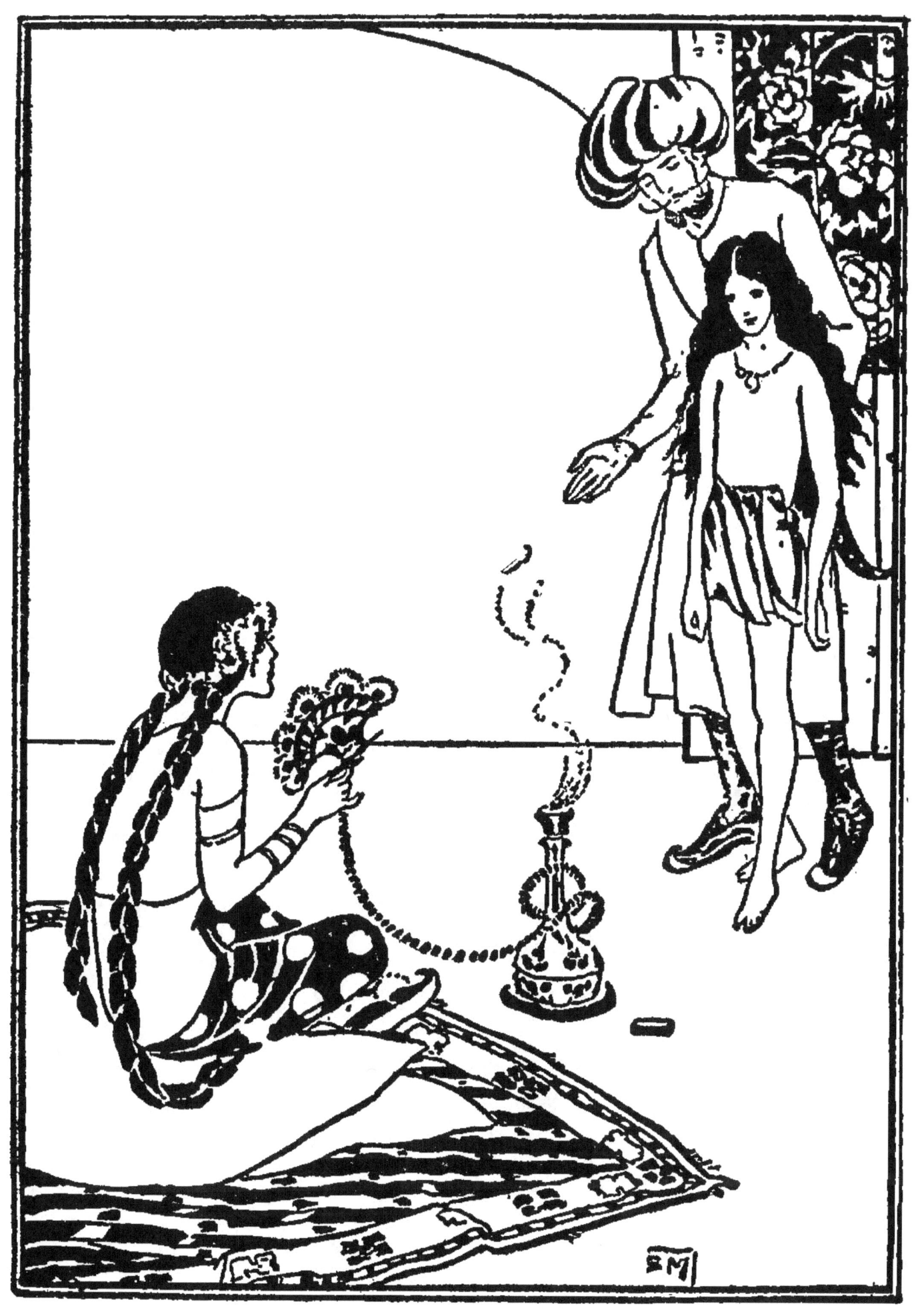

"THE RANEE SAID, 'THIS IS A DEAR LITTLE GIRL.'"

www.ingramcontent.com/pod-product-compliance
Lightning Source LLC
Chambersburg PA
CBHW062210220526
45470CB00009B/2996